THE MAGNIFICENT BOOK OF TREES

THE MAGNIFICENT BOOK OF TREES

ILLUSTRATED BY
Val Walerczuk and Simon Treadwell

WRITTEN BY
Tony Russell

weldonowen

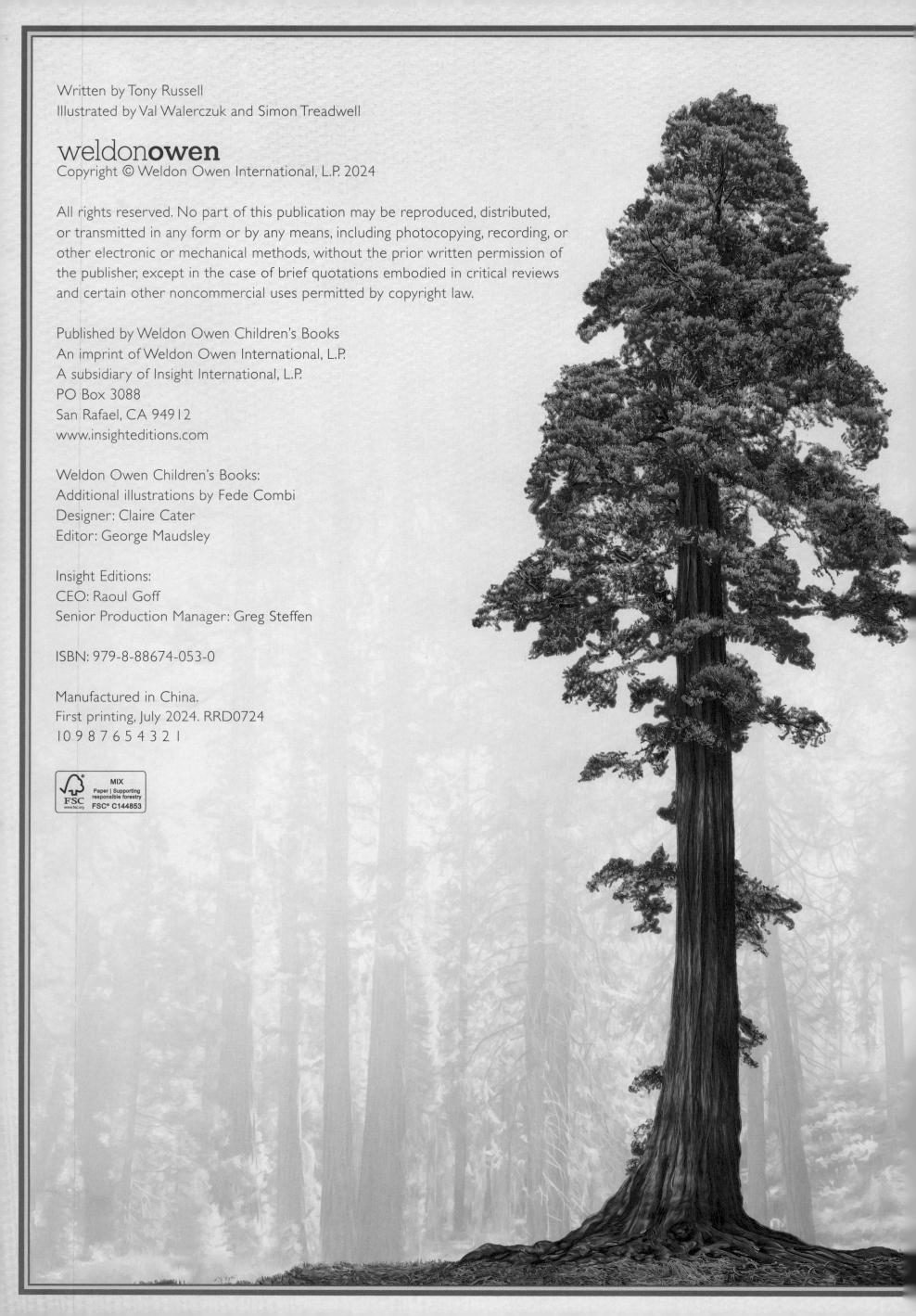

Written by Tony Russell
Illustrated by Val Walerczuk and Simon Treadwell

weldon**owen**

Copyright © Weldon Owen International, L.P. 2024

Published by Weldon Owen Children's Books
An imprint of Weldon Owen International, L.P.
A subsidiary of Insight International, L.P.
PO Box 3088
San Rafael, CA 94912
www.insighteditions.com

Weldon Owen Children's Books:
Additional illustrations by Fede Combi
Designer: Claire Cater
Editor: George Maudsley

Insight Editions:
CEO: Raoul Goff
Senior Production Manager: Greg Steffen

ISBN: 979-8-88674-053-0

Manufactured in China.
First printing, July 2024. RRD0724
10 9 8 7 6 5 4 3 2 1

FSC
www.fsc.org
MIX
Paper | Supporting
responsible forestry
FSC® C144853

Introduction

Trees are the most successful plants on Earth, having survived for 370 million years. Across the world there are roughly 80,000 different species, covering almost one-third of all dry land, from hillsides and mountains to coasts, riversides, and forests, where they collect in their billions.

Trees are essential to all life on Earth. They absorb vast amounts of carbon dioxide from the atmosphere, replacing it with oxygen for animals to breathe. This helps create a liveable planet by reducing pollution and keeping global temperatures stable. Trees influence weather patterns by releasing water vapor, which increases humidity and brings much-needed rain to drier parts of the world. They offer homes to countless species of wildlife. Yet more than 10 percent of the world's trees are endangered in the wild.

The Magnificent Book of Trees is a celebration of trees in all their incredible forms. Marvel at the towering giant redwood—the world's most massive tree—and see how a strangler fig consumes whatever it touches. Spot the animals that call these trees their homes, and learn about the dragon's blood tree, which oozes a blood-red sap. See the rainbow eucalyptus with its multicolored bark and a Japanese cherry tree in full bloom. Discover the world's longest-lived tree, and find out which tree was thought long extinct, which kind of tree was eaten by dinosaurs, and which tree's beans are used to make chocolate.

Embark on a journey into the magnificent realm of trees as you explore some of the most fascinating species from across the world.

Fact file

Found: California, USA

Habitat: Mountains

Height: 160–280 ft (50–85 m)

Trunk width: 20–29 ft (6–8.8 m)

Life span: Up to 3,500 years

Leaves: Evergreen

Contents

Dragon's blood tree

Dracaena draco

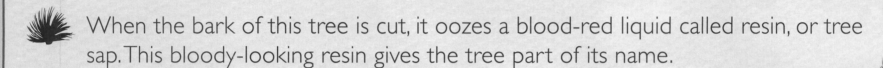 When the bark of this tree is cut, it oozes a blood-red liquid called resin, or tree sap. This bloody-looking resin gives the tree part of its name.

This tree's resin is collected, dried, and used to color the wood of other trees. It is sometimes even used to give the wood of violins a reddish appearance.

It is thought that dragon's blood resin might have been used to make the red paint found in some early human cave paintings in southern Europe.

Scientists class the dragon's blood as a tree, but it is also a part of the asparagus family.

Fact file

Found: Canary Islands, Madeira, Cape Verde, Morocco

Habitat: Hot, dry desertlike

Height: Up to 50 ft (15 m)

Trunk width: Up to 20 ft (5 m)

Life span: 400–600 years

Leaves: Evergreen, palmlike

Most dragon's blood trees live for a few hundred years. One at Icod on the island of Tenerife, though, is believed to be more than 800 years old. It is a symbol of Tenerife and has been used on banknotes and in local coats of arms.

 The fruit grown by dragon's blood trees look like small orange tomatoes. They are said to have a similar taste to tomatoes, too!

Maidenhair

Ginkgo biloba

- The maidenhair, or ginkgo, is the last survivor of an ancient group of trees that lived before and during the time of the dinosaurs.

- There are ginkgo fossils that are more than 170 million years old. They tell us that these trees once grew from the Arctic Circle to the Mediterranean, and from North America to China. They are now endangered.

- In the Jurassic period, ginkgo trees provided both shade and food for dinosaurs, who ate the leaves and seeds. They may have been attracted by the strong smell of the seeds.

- Today there are thought to be no ginkgo trees growing in the wild. All the trees we know about have been planted by humans.

- The distinctive fan-shaped leaves of this tree are similar to those of the maidenhair fern. This is why it is known as the maidenhair tree. The leaves only turn yellow in autumn.

- The maidenhair's leaves and bark taste very bitter. This means they do not have many pest problems compared to other trees.

- Ginkgo trees are good at tolerating air pollution. They are now widely planted by roads and in towns and cities because of their ability to survive where air quality is poor.

Fact file

Found: China

Habitat: Forests

Height: 65–130 ft (20–40 m)

Trunk width: 10 ft (3 m)

Life span: 2,500 years

Leaves: Deciduous

Japanese cherry

Prunus serrulata

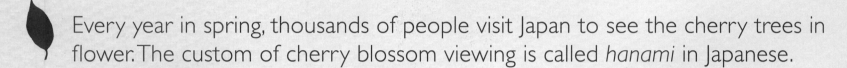

- Every year in spring, thousands of people visit Japan to see the cherry trees in flower. The custom of cherry blossom viewing is called *hanami* in Japanese.

- This tree is considered one of the most beautiful in the world for its bright pink blossom, which lasts for no more than two weeks at a time.

- There are more than 200 different types of flowering cherry trees. Some have white instead of pink blossom.

Fact file

Found: Japan

Habitat: Hillsides, valley woodlands

Height: Up to 22 ft (7 m)

Trunk width: Up to 20 in (50 cm)

Life span: 80–100 years

Leaves: Deciduous

Cherry blossom has been shown in Japanese paintings for centuries, and celebrated in poetry for more than 1,000 years.. The flowers have also long been used as designs for wallpaper and clothing, and today are even used as decorations on cakes and sweets.

 In spring, the flowers are picked and used to make a tea. This is drunk at weddings and other occasions representing new beginnings.

Mangrove

Rhizophora sp.

Mangroves have an ability very few other trees on Earth have. They survive in salty water, including the sea, where most other trees die.

Each mangrove tree contains its own desalination plant. This means it can filter out all the salt from the water it absorbs so it only uses fresh water.

Mangrove forests are important in fighting climate change. During photosynthesis, the process by which plants make food, they suck up the greenhouse gas carbon dioxide. They store huge amounts of the carbon in their soil, leaves, and branches, helping to keep it out of the atmosphere.

This tree's root systems provide important habitats for a rich variety of marine wildlife. Tiny fish, shellfish, and even massive saltwater crocodiles can shelter, live, and hunt among the mangroves.

Mangroves protect some coastal coral reefs by trapping harmful pollutants in their soil. This stops the pollutants from reaching the vulnerable coral.

Fact file

Found: Tropics and subtropics worldwide

Habitat: Coasts, tidal rivers

Height: Up to 80 ft (25 m)

Trunk width: 24 in (60 cm)

Life span: Up to 100 years

Leaves: Evergreen

These trees act as natural barriers to waves and wind, helping defend against storms, floods, and tsunamis. Their roots also hold soil and sediments in place, protecting coastlines from being washed away by the tides.

15

Jacaranda

Jacaranda mimosifolia

 This tree is native in just a few tropical regions of South America. Its unusual lilac flowers have led to it being widely planted in many other places, including South Africa, Australia, and the southern US.

 The city of Pretoria in South Africa is known as Jacaranda City. Thousands of jacarandas have been planted in its streets, gardens, and parks.

 In Queensland, Australia, "purple panic" is said to take hold when students are studying for their exams. This is because it is also the time the jacaranda's purple flowers bloom.

 The jacaranda's thin, pale bark is smooth when the tree is young. As it ages, it becomes more scaly.

 Logging and clearing land for farming are threatening this tree. It is listed as vulnerable by the United Nations.

Fact file

Found: Argentina, Bolivia, Brazil

Habitat: Savannah

Height: Up to 50 ft (15 m)

Trunk width: Up to 3 ft (1 m)

Life span: 150 years

Leaves: Deciduous

In some countries, including South Africa, the woody, tortoise-shaped seed pods of the jacaranda are gathered and used as Christmas tree decorations.

Common oak

Quercus robur

- The common oak is one of more than 600 types of oak tree. Most oaks, including the common oak, are deciduous, but some are evergreen.

- Each oak tree produces around 10 million oak seeds, or acorns, during its lifetime. But only one in every 10,000 will grow to be an adult tree.

- Oak trees are important homes for wildlife. Hundreds of different types of insect live and feed on oaks, while birds help spread the trees' acorns.

- Many oak trees are more than 500 years old, and some live to be more than 1,000 years old.

- Acorns can be ground down to make a type of flour. They have also been used to make "oak coffee."

- Large, spherical growths on oak trees, caused by gall wasps laying their eggs in the trees, were once used to make ink for many important documents.

Fact file

Found: Europe, western Asia

Habitat: Woodland, edges of waterways

Height: Up to 130 ft (40 m)

Trunk width: 36 ft (11 m)

Life span: 500 years

Leaves: Deciduous

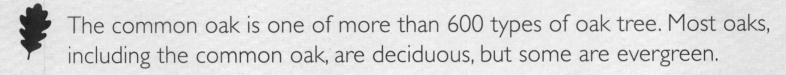

Oak timber is strong and does not rot easily. It has been used to make many things over the centuries, including ships, buildings, and barrels.

Serbian spruce

Picea omorika

This narrow evergreen conifer tree comes from a very snowy area in Serbia and Bosnia called the Drina Valley.

The Serbian spruce has developed this shape so snow cannot weigh heavily on its branches and break them. Instead, it slides off the sides and onto the ground.

Once there were lots of Serbian spruce growing in the wild, but now it is so rare that it is feared it may soon become extinct. Many have been cut down for their timber or destroyed by wildfires.

Serbian spruce is a very popular tree for growing in parks and gardens across the world because of its unusual shape.

Some Serbian spruce are grown as Christmas trees. This is because of its similarity to other Christmas tree species, such as the Norway spruce and some fir and pine trees.

This tree has purple-brown cones. They are eaten by squirrels, mice, and many small birds, including finches and tits.

Before the last Ice Age, Serbian spruce grew all the way across Europe, from Russia to Ireland.

Fact file

Found: Serbia, Bosnia

Habitat: Mountainsides

Height: 70 ft (21 m)

Trunk width: 3 ft (1 m)

Life span: 80–100 years

Leaves: Evergreen

African baobab

Adansonia digitata

- African baobabs grow on the hot savannah. Their presence in the dry conditions shows there must be water somewhere nearby.

- With its large, round trunk and branches that look just like tree roots, the baobab has been nicknamed the upside-down tree.

- These trees are known for their huge silver-gray trunks, which are full of thousands of gallons of water.

- Baobab trees drop their leaves in the dry season. They remain leafless for eight months of every year.

Fact file

Found: Africa, Madagascar, Yemen, Oman

Habitat: Savannah

Height: 16–82 ft (5–25 m)

Trunk width: 33–46 ft (10–14 m)

Life span: More than 2,000 years

Leaves: Deciduous

Elephants like to eat baobab leaves, which taste a little like spinach.

 As the temperature on the savannah drops later in the day, the baobab's white flowers begin to open. They stay open for just one night, and are pollinated by visiting fruit bats.

 Quite often, large, old baobab tree trunks become hollow. In the past, the hollow trees were used by people as houses, bars, and even a prison!

Sweet chestnut

Castanea sativa

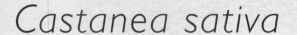 Sweet chestnut is a long-lived tree related to oak. It produces long, narrow, creamy-yellow spikes with a fragrant scent.

This sweet chestnut is one of the last trees in the northern hemisphere to flower each year, usually in July.

The tree's brown, shiny seeds are known as chestnuts. They are often roasted and sold as food in winter, and have been used in cooking for centuries.

Sweet chestnut seeds are eaten by squirrels, mice, and deer. The animals gorge on the nuts in autumn as they build up fat reserves to survive the winter.

The oldest known sweet chestnut is called the Hundred Horse Chestnut. It lives on Mount Etna in Sicily, and is thought to be between 2,000 and 4,000 years old.

Fact file

Found: Mediterranean, southern Europe, southwest Asia

Habitat: Woodlands

Height: 100–115 ft (30–35 m)

Trunk width: 5–15 ft (1.5–4.5 m)

Life span: 500–700 years

Leaves: Deciduous

In parts of Europe, sweet chestnut seeds were once dried and ground up to make a flour for baking bread.

Monkey puzzle

Araucaria araucana

 Monkey puzzle trees got their unusual name because of their spiny, spiraling branches. It was said that climbing them would be a puzzle even for a monkey.

 This evergreen tree only grows wild in a small, 150-square-mile part of the Andes mountain range in South America.

 Farming, forest fires, and logging for this tree's timber mean it is now an endangered species. New types of trees are also taking up more of the monkey puzzles' limited habitat space.

 Monkey puzzles produce male and female cones on the same tree. The female cones are round and start off bright green before turning brown. The male cones are long and drooping.

 During the Jurassic period, 200 million years ago, monkey puzzle trees grew all over the Southern Hemisphere. Their prickly leaves were a popular meal for dinosaurs.

 Female cones release large seeds. The seeds look like brown nuts, which can be eaten by people and animals, and are full of protein.

Fact file

Found: Chile, Argentina

Habitat: Mountain slopes

Height: 100–130 ft (30–40 m)

Trunk width: 3–5 ft (1–1.5 m)

Life span: 1,200 years

Leaves: Evergreen

New Zealand Christmas tree

Metrosideros excelsa

- This tree get its unusual name because its bright red flowers bloom at Christmastime in New Zealand.

- The Māori, the indigenous people of New Zealand, call this type of tree *pohutukawa*. In Māori mythology, its crimson flowers are said to represent the blood of a young warrior who died while trying to avenge his father's death.

- While the tree is known for its deep red flowers, other groups produce pink or yellow blooms.

- The tree is nicknamed the cliff-hugger because it can grow on very steep sea cliffs, where there is very little soil.

Fact file

Found: New Zealand

Habitat: Coastal cliffs

Height: Up to 65 ft (20 m)

Trunk width: Up to 10 ft (3 m)

Life span: 1,000 years

Leaves: Evergreen

Some native New Zealand birds, such as the tui, the stitchbird, and the bellbird rely on the bright red flowers as an important source of nectar. The birds pollinate the flowers while they feed on the nectar.

Threats such as farming and pests have reduced this tree's range. Possums have damaged and even killed some trees by stripping the leaves for food.

This hardy tree can grow on bare ground, including where lava flows have cooled into hard rock.

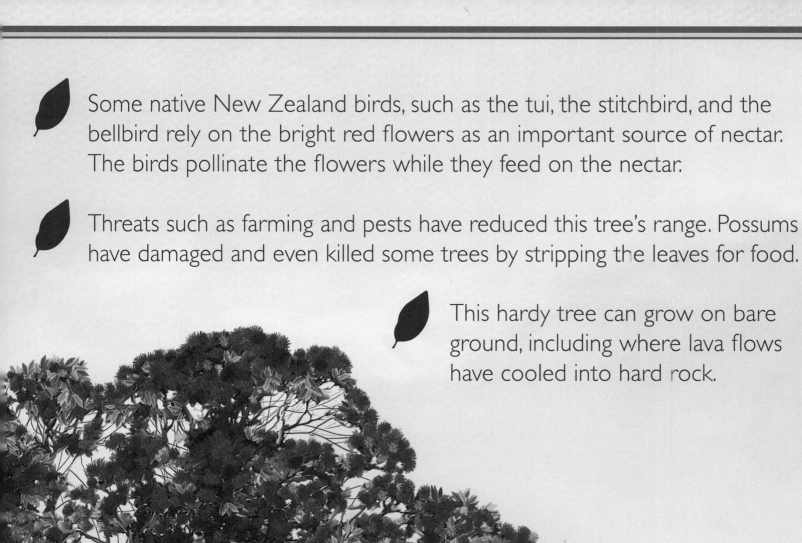

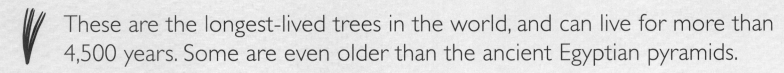

Bristlecone pine

Pinus longaeva

These are the longest-lived trees in the world, and can live for more than 4,500 years. Some are even older than the ancient Egyptian pyramids.

Bristlecone pines can survive on as little as 10 inches (25 centimeters) of rain per year, and can go for months without water. They live in dry, rocky, desertlike conditions.

It can take more than 50 years for these slow growers to reach just 10 feet (three meters) in height. They can eventually grow up to 50 feet (15 meters) tall.

This tree's cones are covered with tiny, sharp prickles, or bristles. These are what gives the bristlecone pine its name.

The branches are home to several American birds, such as mountain chickadees, hermit thrushes, mountain bluebirds, and violet-green swallows. They also provide a safe place for mammals and reptiles, which might eat the birds and their eggs.

The wood of this tree is very durable. Even after a bristlecone pine has died, it can remain standing on its roots for centuries without rotting.

Fact file

Found: Eastern California, Utah, and Nevada, USA

Habitat: Rocky soils in open ground

Height: 16–82 ft (5–25 m)

Trunk width: 33–46 ft (10–14 m)

Life span: More than 2,000 years

Leaves: Evergreen

Yew

Taxus baccata

- Yews are among the oldest living trees on Earth. Some are known to be more than 4,000 years old—that's older than nearly every country in the world.

- Ancient humans such as the Celts and Druids thought yew trees were magical. They believed that if people worshipped them, they would live a long life.

- Chemicals found in a yew's needles, or evergreen leaves, are used by doctors to treat several forms of cancer.

- It is thought every part of the yew is toxic, except for its arils, or bright red berries. If eaten untreated, its poison can be fatal.

- Yews are found in many Christian churches and cemeteries. This is perhaps because they were built on the sites of temples used in pagan religions, for which the yew was sacred.

- The yew's long life and toxic nature mean it has stood for death for centuries. Its branches' ability to take root and and sprout again are one reason it is also a symbol of life and rebirth.

Fact file

Found: Western Europe to western Asia

Habitat: Woodlands

Height: Up to 65 ft (20 m)

Trunk width: Up to 23 ft (7 m)

Life span: 2,000–4,000 years

Leaves: Evergreen

One of the world's oldest surviving wooden artifacts is a spearhead made from yew wood. It is thought to be more than 400,000 years old.

Giant redwood

Sequoiadendron giganteum

➤ Giant redwoods are the largest living trees in the world. The biggest of all is called General Sherman, in Sequoia National Park, California. It weighs around 1,400 tons, which is more than the weight of six blue whales.

➤ These trees have soft, hairy, reddish bark, which can be more than one foot (30 centimeters) thick. The bark acts like a fire blanket, and helps protect the trees from wildfires.

➤ Birds often nest in the bark of redwood trees. Sometimes they use the bark's reddish, hairy fiber to help build their nests.

➤ Fire is vital for these trees to reproduce. The heat from a wildfire causes the trees' cones to open and release their seeds in the wind.

➤ Some of the redwoods growing in California today may be more than 3,500 years old.

The needles, or leaves, of redwood trees can soak up moisture from fog and mist. They turn it into "rain" that falls on the ground beneath the tree.

Redwood bark contains a chemical called tannin. This is what makes the bark look red. Tannin also protects the trees against rot, insects, fungi, and disease so it can live for thousands of years.

Fact file

Found: California, USA

Habitat: Mountains

Height: 160–280 ft (50–85 m)

Trunk width: 20–29 ft (6–8.8 m)

Life span: Up to 3,500 years

Leaves: Evergreen

Cacao

Theobroma cacao

Beans from this tree are used to make one of the world's most popular products—chocolate. The beans are the seeds of the cacao tree, which are stored in the tree's orange or yellow fruit.

Humans have eaten cacao beans for thousands of years. The Mayans and Aztecs mixed ground cacao beans and chile to create a bitter, spicy drink.

Cacao trees begin to produce seeds when they are only four or five years old. The seeds grow in the fruit—long pods that each contain between 30 and 60 seeds.

Today, chocolate made from the cacao mostly comes from trees that have been planted in cacao orchards in Africa and Indonesia, rather than from the rain forest.

The scientific name of the cacao, *Theobroma*, means "food of the gods."

Fact file

Found: Central and South America

Habitat: Tropical rain forests

Height: Up to 26 ft (8 m)

Trunk width: 12 in (30 cm)

Life span: Up to 100 years

Leaves: Evergreen

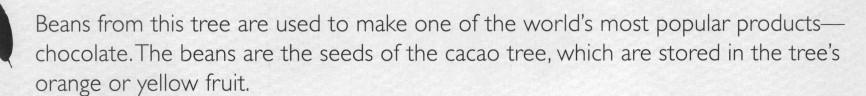

In Mesoamerica, a historical area covering parts of Mexico and Central America, cacao beans were commonly used as money, including by the Aztecs.

Swamp cypress

Taxodium distichum

- Unlike most other conifer trees, the swamp cypress is not evergreen. It drops all its needles, or leaves, every autumn, and is bare until it grows new leaves in the spring. This gives the tree its other name, the bald cypress.

- The swamp cypress grows wild in the Everglades of Florida and the southeastern US, where it can live in water all year round.

- This tree is important for wildlife. Frogs, toads, and salamanders use the spaces between the roots to breed. Wood ducks nest in hollow trunks, raptors such as bald eagles nest in the treetops, and wild turkeys and squirrels eat the tree's seeds.

- An ancient underwater swamp cypress forest was found off the coast of Alabama. The trees are thought to be more than 50,000 years old, and are so well preserved they still smell of fresh cypress sap when they are cut.

Fact file

Found: Southeast USA

Habitat: Wetlands, floodplains, swamps

Height: Up to 160 ft (50 m)

Trunk width: Up to 5 ft (1.5 m)

Life span: 200–1,000 years

Leaves: Deciduous

In places where the ground is very wet, these trees grow "knees," or upright roots, above the ground. Scientists are still trying to work out the purpose of the knees.

Umbrella pine

Pinus pinea

 The umbrella-shaped canopy of these trees can be spotted up and down the coastlines of parts of Spain, France, and Italy. Their wide-spreading branches offer shade from the hot Mediterranean sun, like an umbrella, and together with their shape give these trees their name.

 Umbrella pines were planted alongside old Roman roads in southern Europe. They would have provided protection from the Sun to Roman soldiers as they marched across their empire.

 Conservationists plant these trees in sand dunes and near the sea to defend coastlines from erosion. Their roots bind the soil and sand together, keeping it from easily washing away in high tides or flooding.

 The hard shell that surrounds the umbrella pine's seeds give this tree its other name, the stone pine.

 The umbrella pine's seeds are known as pine nuts. These can be eaten, and have been collected as food by humans since prehistoric times.

Fact file

Found: Mediterranean

Habitat: Low, coastal hills

Height: 40–65 ft (12–20 m)

Trunk width: Up to 3 ft (1 m)

Life span: Up to 300 years

Leaves: Evergreen

Umbrella pines are popular as bonsai trees. Bonsai are miniature versions of trees grown in containers, which are carefully trimmed to look beautiful.

Japanese cedar

Cryptomeria japonica

➤ The Japanese name for this tree is *sugi*, which means pure and clean. Perhaps this is why the tree is often planted close to Japanese Buddhist temples and shrines.

➤ An old Japanese tradition was to plant a *sugi* tree when a baby girl was born. When the girl was old enough to marry, the tree would be cut down and the timber used to make a box. The girl would pack all her possessions in the box to take to her new home.

➤ The world's longest avenue of trees is planted with Japanese cedars. It is in the city of Nikko in Japan, and is around 22 miles (35 kilometers) long.

➤ Japanese cedar wood is highly valued. It is strong, durable, and insect-resistant, and has a scent thought by some to smell of oranges and lemons.

➤ Strips of the Japanese cedar's fragant red bark are sometimes burnt as incense.

This tree's leaves are an important food source for the caterpillars of several different kinds of moth.

The oldest known Japanese cedar is called Jōmon Sugi. It is located on the island of Yakushima and is thought to be between 2,170 and 7,200 years old—that's older than the country of Japan itself!

Fact file

Found: Japan, naturalized in China

Habitat: Forests

Height: Up to 230 ft (70 m)

Trunk width: Up to 13 ft (4 m)

Life span: 800–1,000 years

Leaves: Evergreen

Cork oak

Quercus suber

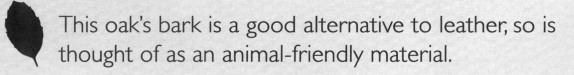 This type of oak is famed for its magnificent bark, which is the source of the material cork.

Cork oak bark can be cut and stripped from the trunk of a tree to make cork once it reaches 25 years old. This does not harm the tree. It will regrow its bark, which can be removed again nine to 12 years later. Each tree can have its bark stripped around 15 times.

This oak's bark is a good alternative to leather, so is thought of as an animal-friendly material.

Cork bark is water-resistant and full of pockets of air. This allows it to float. It is often used to help people learning to swim!

The cork oak is the national tree of Portugal. It is against the law there to cut down a cork oak without a license.

Fact file

Found: Western Mediterranean, North Africa, southwest Europe

Habitat: Hilly open woodland

Height: 32–82 ft (10–25 m)

Trunk width: Up to 6 ft (1.8 m)

Life span: 200 years

Leaves: Evergreen

Cork oaks can live through long periods of drought. Its bark is resistant to heat and can protect the tree from forest fires.

Flamboyant tree

Delonix regia

 This striking tree has been planted far beyond its natural range for its striking bright red flowers. It is now found in many tropical and subtropical regions of the world, especially to decorate streets, town squares, and parks.

 The flamboyant tree is part of the pea or bean family. Members of this family of plants are called legumes.

 After flowering, the tree produces long, soft, green bean pods, which contain the tree's seeds. As they age, they turn dark brown and woody. The pods can be up to 24 inches (60 centimeters) long.

Fact file

Found: Madagascar

Habitat: Deciduous forests

Height: Up to 40 ft (12 m)

Trunk width: 5 ft (1.5 m)

Life span: 50 years or more

Leaves: Deciduous

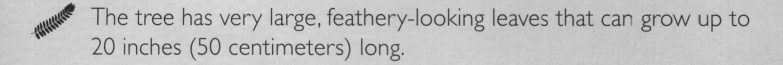 The tree has very large, feathery-looking leaves that can grow up to 20 inches (50 centimeters) long.

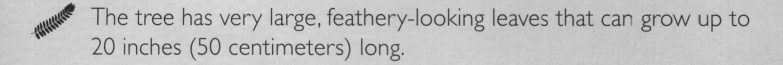 While the flamboyant tree is known for the redness of its petals, one rare variety grows deep-yellow flowers.

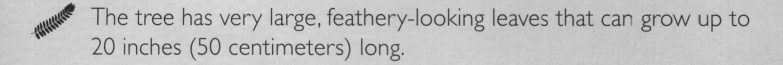 When this tree's pods have hardened with age, the beans inside rattle when shaken. The pods are often given to babies and young children to play with as toys.

Oriental plane

Platanus orientalis

 This tree is best known for its light-gray bark. The bark flakes off as it ages, revealing cream and pink patches beneath.

 Oriental planes can live for hundreds of years. As they age, their trunks can grow to more than 13 feet (four meters) wide.

 The Roman author Pliny the Elder wrote about the many medicines made from the bark, leaves, and sap of this tree. He believed these remedies could be used for burns, bites, infections, and stings.

 Plane trees can withstand high levels of air pollution. They shed strips of their bark to rid themselves of pollutants, pests, mosses, or fungus.

 Hippocrates, the Father of Medicine, taught medical students in the shade of a plane tree on the Greek island of Kos nearly 2,500 years ago. A tree there today is said to be a descendant of Hippocrates' tree.

Fact file

Found: Southeast Europe to India

Habitat: River valleys, ravines

Height: Up to 100 ft (30 m)

Trunk width: Up to 13 ft (4 m)

Life span: Over 500 years

Leaves: Deciduous

Buddha tree

Ficus religiosa

- The Buddha tree, or bo tree, is one of the most sacred types of tree in the world. It is important to both Hindus and Buddhists.

- This species is thought to have been the one that the Buddha sat under when he gained enlightenment almost 2,500 years ago.

- This tree is a member of the fig family. It is also known as a banyan or strangler fig.

- Strangler fig flowers are pollinated by the fig wasp. The wasp transfers pollen as it crawls into the flowers to look for a place to lay its eggs.

- The Buddha tree's leaves are said to give pain relief from some types of snakebites.

Strangler figs start life as a seed dropped by an animal high in another type of tree. The seed grows roots, which snake along the tree and down to the ground, where they enter the soil. As the roots thicken, they tighten around the tree, strangling it and allowing the fig to take over.

The tree is used for many different things. The small seeds are sometimes dried and threaded onto necklaces, and the bark can be used to make a red pigment for dying cloth.

Fact file

Found: Southeast Asia

Habitat: Tropical rain forests

Height: 50–100 ft (15–30 m)

Trunk width: 23–33 ft (7–10 m)

Life span: 2,000 years

Leaves: Deciduous

Lebanon cedar

Cedrus libani

 This tree is known for its wide-spreading branches. It grows wild from Lebanon to Turkey.

 The Lebanon cedar's wood was valued by the Phoenicians and other ancient civilizations for its use in shipbuilding. Long ago, the Phoenicians were the inhabitants of Lebanon and were famous for being great sailors.

 This species of cedar is the national symbol of Lebanon, and appears on its flag and coat of arms.

 The oil in cedar wood gives it a strong, earthy smell. The wood works as a natural insect repellent, and is used to protect clothes from bug and moth bites.

 In the Bible, King Solomon used this tree's wood to build the Temple in Jerusalem, nearly 3,000 years ago.

Fact file

Found: Eastern Mediterranean

Habitat: Mountainsides, valleys

Height: Up to 130 ft (40 m)

Trunk width: Up to 13 ft (4 m)

Life span: 1,000 years

Leaves: Evergreen

As these trees age, cracks and openings develop in their trunks and branches. They provide nesting and roosting places for birds, owls, and bats.

Silver birch

Betula pendula

Silver birch gets its name from its silvery-white bark.

The tree is known as a pioneer tree. This means it is one of the first trees able to grow on bare or fire-swept ground.

These trees have thin, cylinder-shaped male and female flowers called catkins. The female catkins are full of tiny, winged seeds, which are scattered far and wide by the wind.

The silver birch's fine twigs used to be made into broom heads. They were known as besom brooms, and looked like the brooms witches fly on in stories.

Silver birches are important for conservation and the environment. More than 500 different butterflies, moths, and other insects have been found on them.

Silver birch trees have small leaves and light branches. This allows sunlight to reach the ground below, encouraging flowers such as bluebells, primroses, and wood anemones to grow.

Fact file

Found: Europe, Asia

Habitat: Hills, mountains, moorland, heathland

Height: 80 ft (15–25 m)

Trunk width: 24 in (60 cm)

Life span: 80–100 years

Leaves: Deciduous

Many birds are found in silver birch woodlands, including chaffinches, willow warblers, nightingales, robins, and woodpeckers.

Kapok

Ceiba pentandra

 This rain forest giant is known for its remarkable seed pods. The pods contain a fluffy material that looks a bit like woolly cotton candy.

 Kapoks live from southern Mexico to the southern Amazon, as well in West Africa. Some experts think they found their way to Africa because their seeds floated across the Atlantic and were able to establish a home there.

 The kapok tree is huge. It is supported by massive outgrowths from the trunk called buttresses. The buttresses can reach more than 30 feet (10 meters) up the trunk.

 This tree's trunk is covered in prickly thorns. They prevent animals from eating the kapok's thin bark.

 The kapok's creamy-white flowers bloom at night, and give off a strong scent that attracts bats. As the bats move between the flowers to get at the nectar, they transfer the pollen on their fur to the flowers, pollinating them.

Fact file

Found: Central and South America, Caribbean, West Africa

Habitat: Tropical and subtropical rain forest

Height: Up to 200 ft (60 m)

Trunk width: Up to 16 ft (5 m)

Life span: Up to 500 years

Leaves: Deciduous

The fluff inside kapok seed pods was once used to stuff such things as pillows, life jackets, and teddy bears. It is now sometimes used in insulation in homes.

Italian cypress

Cupressus sempervirens

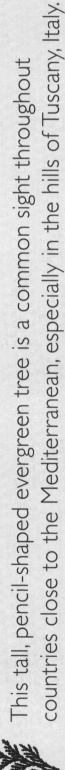

This tall, pencil-shaped evergreen tree is a common sight throughout countries close to the Mediterranean, especially in the hills of Tuscany, Italy.

Italian cypress is popular for its unusual shape, and has been widely planted, especially alongside roads and paths.

The tree has represented grief and mourning since ancient times, and is often grown in and around cemeteries. As a result, it has been known as the tree of mourning or the churchyard cypress in different cultures.

This tree's timber is the traditional wood used to make Italian harpsichords and other keyboard instruments.

It is said the doors of the old St. Peter's Basilica in what is now the Vatican City in Rome were made from Italian cypress timber. They are thought to have stood for more than a thousand years before the new church was built.

The Italian cypress's seeds are stored in its cones. The cones sometimes stay sealed on the tree for years. The heat from wildfires may open the cones, causing the seeds to be spread.

In Roman mythology, a boy called Cyparrisus was turned into a cypress. After accidentally killing a tame stag, his grief was so strong that he asked the gods to be able to mourn forever. He was transformed into an Italian cypress, with the tree's sap being his endless tears.

Fact file

Found: Mediterrranean, North Africa

Habitat: Dry hills and mountainsides

Height: 65–130 ft (20–40 m)

Trunk width: 3 ft (1 m)

Life span: Up to 1,000 years

Leaves: Evergreen

Tibetan cherry

Prunus serrula

- This small tree grows way up in the Himalayan Mountains. It can live up to 12,000 feet (3,700 meters) above sea level.

- Climbers readying themselves to scale Mount Everest can see this tree growing alongside the footpath to Everest Base Camp.

- Tibetan cherry has shiny mahogany-red bark. It looks like it has been polished. It is particularly easy to see against the snow in the Himalayas.

- The Tibetan cherry is very tolerant of pollution in the atmosphere. This is why it is so often planted in towns and cities, where pollution is usually higher.

- The tree grows clusters of white flowers among the emerging leaves in spring, and small cherry fruits in late summer. In autumn, its leaves turn yellow.

- A dark gray or green dye can be drawn from the tree's leaves and fruit.

Fact file

Found: Nepal, western China

Habitat: Mountain forests, hillsides

Height: Up to 26 ft (8 m)

Trunk width: 24 in (60 cm)

Life span: Up to 50 years

Leaves: Deciduous

As this tree gets older, its shiny bark peels away in bands. Its peeling bark gives it the nickname of paperback cherry because the strips of the thin bark used to be used as paper to write upon.

Tree rhododendron

Rhododendron arboreum

All rhododendrons are shrubs rather than trees, but this species grows more like a tree, with some reaching up to nearly 60 feet (20 meters) in height. Their long, spreading branches could cover a tennis court.

Tree rhododendrons are native to the Himalayas, where they are found up to 10,000 feet (3,000 meters) above sea level.

The tree's big, deep pink or red flowers open in early spring while the surrounding mountains are still covered in snow.

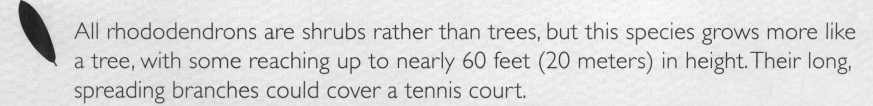

Fact file

Found: Himalayas

Habitat: Mountain foothills

Height: Up to 60 ft (18 m)

Trunk width: 6 ft (1.5 m)

Life span: 300 years

Leaves: Evergreen

In the Himalayas, rhododendron petals are dried and used to make a tea. The drink is said to be good for treating digestive problems and other health issues.

Himalayan bees use the nectar from tree rhododendrons to make honey. Some Nepalese sherpa families are beekeepers, and sell the honey they harvest in markets and teahouses to tourists on the trail to the high Himalayan peaks.

Joshua tree

Yucca brevifolia

 Although it is as big as a tree, the Joshua tree is not really a tree at all. It is the world's largest type of yucca plant.

 Joshua trees can survive a long time without rain. This is because they grow long roots of up to 33 feet (10 meters), which go deep underground to find hidden pockets of water.

 A Joshua tree's flowers and branches provide food and shelter for many desert animals and birds. This includes the desert tortoise, the ladder-backed woodpecker, and the red-shafted flicker bird, which builds nests in the tree.

 It is thought that the Joshua tree was given its name by Mormon settlers crossing the Mojave Desert in the mid-1800s. The shape of the tree reminded them of the biblical story of Joshua reaching his hands up to the sky in prayer.

 Joshua trees are very slow growing, and may only grow around 1 inch (2.5 centimeters) each year. This means they can take between 75 and 100 years to reach their full height.

Fact file

Found: Mojave Desert of California, Nevada, Utah, and Arizona, USA; Mexico

Habitat: Desert

Height: Up to 40 ft (12 m)

Trunk width: 3–5 ft (1–1.5 m)

Life span: 1,200 years

Leaves: Evergreen

Brazil nut

Bertholletia excelsa

This tree is one of the tallest in the Amazon rain forest. Its wide crown can be seen rising above the rest of the forest canopy.

Fruit on this tree only grows in unspoiled forest. The bees that pollinate the tree are not found in areas where some trees have been cut down, so the tree cannot produce any more nuts there.

Only the agouti, a large rodent, has teeth strong enough to break into the hard pods of the Brazil nut tree.

The tree's nuts are contained in a hard, round, heavy pod. A pod is about the size of a large orange and contains up to 24 nuts.

The Brazil nut tree's creamy-white flowers can only be pollinated by a few types of bee. Once pollinated, the flowers are able to grow the fruit that give this tree its name—Brazil nuts.

Deforestation for roadbuilding and farmland is threatening this tree. Overharvesting of the tree's nuts by agoutis and humans is also reducing the number of young trees growing.

Fact file

Found: South America

Habitat: River edges, rain forest

Height: Up to 160 ft (50 m)

Trunk width: 3–6½ ft (1–2 m)

Life span: 500 years

Leaves: Deciduous

Rowan

Sorbus aucuparia

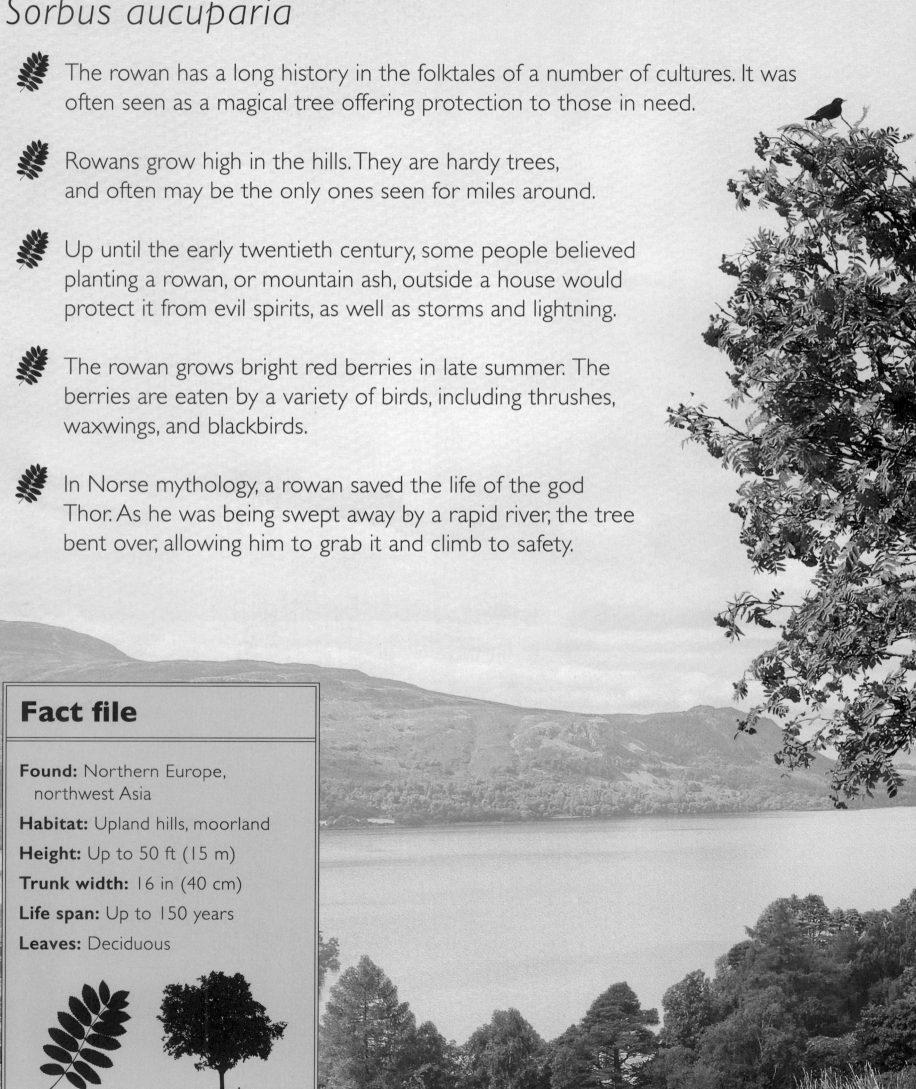

The rowan has a long history in the folktales of a number of cultures. It was often seen as a magical tree offering protection to those in need.

Rowans grow high in the hills. They are hardy trees, and often may be the only ones seen for miles around.

Up until the early twentieth century, some people believed planting a rowan, or mountain ash, outside a house would protect it from evil spirits, as well as storms and lightning.

The rowan grows bright red berries in late summer. The berries are eaten by a variety of birds, including thrushes, waxwings, and blackbirds.

In Norse mythology, a rowan saved the life of the god Thor. As he was being swept away by a rapid river, the tree bent over, allowing him to grab it and climb to safety.

Fact file

Found: Northern Europe, northwest Asia

Habitat: Upland hills, moorland

Height: Up to 50 ft (15 m)

Trunk width: 16 in (40 cm)

Life span: Up to 150 years

Leaves: Deciduous

Another name for the rowan was the traveler's tree. It was said to prevent those on a journey from becoming lost.

Wollemi pine

Wollemia nobilis

 The Wollemi pine is a tree that has risen from the dead. It was thought to have been extinct on Earth for over two million years. But in 1994, a grove of around 100 living trees was found in a hidden canyon in Australia.

 When the Wollemi pine was discovered, it could only be identified by using fossils from long-extinct conifers because it is such an unusual tree.

 While the tree is called a pine, it is not a true pine or a member of the wider pine family. It is part of the araucarian family.

 These trees are critically endangered. Their location is kept a secret to protect the very few living wild trees from diseases and destruction that might be brought by visitors.

 The small group of living Wollemi pines were threatened by the damaging Australian bushfire season of 2019–2020. They were saved by specialist firefighters using aircraft to drop water and fire-resistant liquids.

 As this tree ages, it grows brown bobbles on its bark. They look a bit like a children's puffed rice cereal.

The tree's male cones are long, thin and orange. The female cones are small, green ball shapes covered with bristles.

Fact file

Found: Australia

Habitat: Temperate rain forest

Height: Up to 130 ft (40 m)

Trunk width: 3 ft (1 m)

Life span: More than 500 years

Leaves: Evergreen

Magnolia

Magnolia sp.

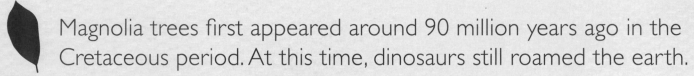

Magnolia trees first appeared around 90 million years ago in the Cretaceous period. At this time, dinosaurs still roamed the earth.

These types of tree were some of the first to produce what we recognize as flowers. Earlier flowering trees did not have petals.

Flying beetles are attracted by a magnolia's colorful petals. Covered in pollen after visits to other flowers, they crawl inside the magnolia flower on the hunt for nectar. As they feed, the pollen on them is transferred to the flower, pollinating the magnolia.

The magnolia's pink or white flowers can grow to huge sizes of up to 14 inches (35 centimeters) across. That's wider than a basketball!

This tree's bark is sometimes ground up and used in making toothpaste.

Fact file

Found: Asia, North America

Habitat: Damp woodlands

Height: Up to 100 ft (30 m)

Trunk width: Up to 8 ft (2.5 m)

Life span: 200 years

Leaves: Deciduous

Olive

Olea europaea

Olive trees have been planted throughout warmer regions of the world for thousands of years. Their nutritious fruit and the oil harvested from them have made these trees important to many different cultures.

These evergreen trees have thick trunks that continue to grow as they age.

The olive branch has stood for peace for at least 2,500 years. It appears on many flags, and a small gold replica was even left on the Moon by astronaut Neil Armstrong in 1969 as a call for peace on Earth.

Olive trees have been grown for their fruit in Greece for 4,000 years. In ancient times, the oil made from the olives was used to anoint, or bless, kings and athletes.

Today, more than 800 million olive trees can be found across the world.

In ancient Greece, temples were often illuminated by the glow from lamps burning olive oil. The golden liquid was also used for the eternal flame of the original Olympic Games in Greece.

Fact file

Found: Mediterranean

Habitat: Dry, open land

Height: 26–52 ft (8–15 m)

Trunk width: Up to 10 ft (3 m)

Life span: 2,000 years

Leaves: Evergreen

Winning athletes at the ancient Olympic Games were crowned with a wreath of olive leaves. These were taken from a special wild olive tree that grew at Olympia, said to have been planted by the hero Heracles.

These trees are very hardy. They survive long droughts, and are resistant to wildfires and disease.

Rainbow eucalyptus

Eucalyptus deglupta

 The rainbow eucalyptus is a giant of the rain forest. It grows higher than any other type of eucalyptus, with some having reached 250 feet (76 meters) tall.

 This is the only type of eucalyptus to live in rain forest or in the Northern Hemisphere.

 These trees are very fast growers. They can sometimes grow up to six feet (two meters) in a year.

 The tree is known for its multicolored bark. Old bark sheds in strips in summer, revealing a different color beneath. The youngest bark is lime green, which turns orange, red, purple, and blue as it ages.

Oil produced by eucalyptus leaves is used by people for various breathing problems, including coughs and colds.

In the Philippines, this tree is grown for pulpwood. This is timber that is used in making white paper.

Fact file

Found: Philippines, Indonesia, Papua New Guinea

Habitat: Tropical rain forest

Height: Up to 200 ft (60 m)

Trunk width: 8 ft (2.5 m)

Life span: Up to 150 years

Leaves: Evergreen, palmlike

Japanese maple

Acer palmatum

 In autumn, this tree's leaves turn a variety of colors, from fiery red to yellow, before drifting to the ground. The leaves are green in spring and summer.

 Japanese maples have been grown in gardens and temples in Japan for centuries. In recent times, they have become popular for their rich leaf color. This has seen them planted across the world, from North America to New Zealand.

 The tree produces fruits called samaras. These are small, papery, wing-shaped pods containing the tree's seeds. Their shape allows the samara to spin as it falls, carrying the seeds away from the parent tree on the wind.

 In Japan, planting these trees is part of gardening as an art form. They are prized for the intricate shapes of their branches even in winter, as well their changing color through the year.

 There are more than 1,000 types of Japanese maple. Their leaves vary from broad and handlike to more fernlike, but they all come from the same species of tree, *Acer palmatum*.

Fact file

Found: Japan, Korea, China, Mongolia, Russia

Habitat: Woodlands

Height: 20–33 ft (6–10 m)

Trunk width: 24 in (60 cm)

Life span: 150 years

Leaves: Deciduous

This tree's leaves are sometimes eaten as a snack. In Osaka Prefecture, they are covered in a sweet butter and fried before being served.

 Japanese maples are often cultivated as bonsai, or dwarf trees, in pots and containers. Bonsai can live to be hundreds of years old, yet not grow as tall as a human adult.

Trees Around the World

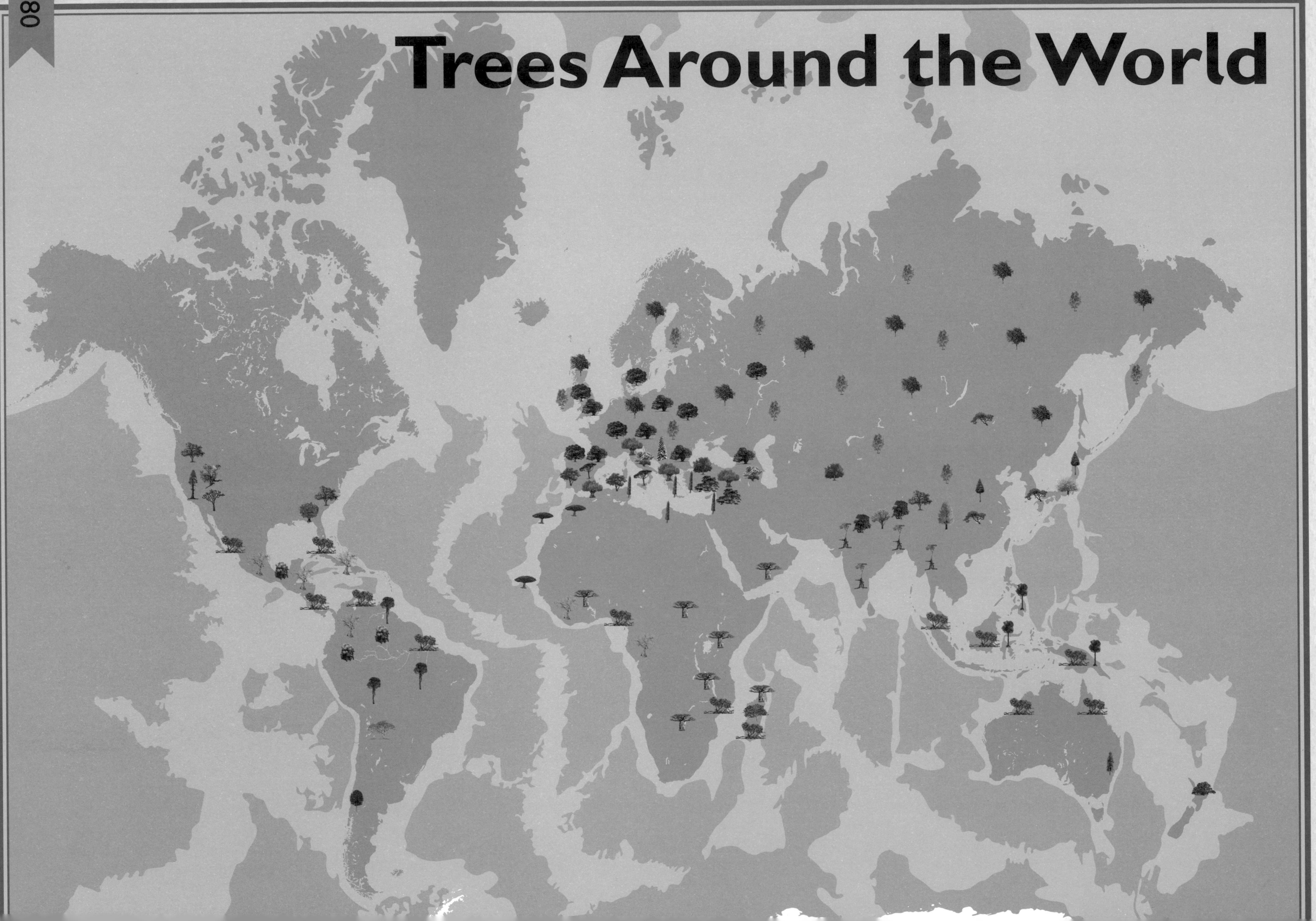